Cycle Touring for Beginners

Copyright Roy Everitt 2014-2018. All rights reserved.

You Really Can Become a Cycle Tourist in Six Weeks or Less

Spring, when the clocks go forward and we can once again enjoy the lighter evenings, is the very best time to start your preparations for an early summer challenge or adventure, a midsummer all-nighter or a once in a lifetime tour. For me, the anticipation (or the memory) of a tour is what dreams are made of.

But, if you want to get fitter, and especially cycling fit, the best time to start is always now.

Whatever your plans and ambitions, this book will help you achieve them, just as it has helped many people already.

Long winter nights, disappointing spring days and any time the weather turns nasty will always make me long for those blue remembered days spent soaking up the scenery, the sunshine (mostly) and the adventurous spirit of an epic trip that might easily have never happened, followed by another that was no less wonderful for not being the first.

All kinds of things conspire to give us opportunities, challenges and once in a lifetime adventures, but if you want to start making your own luck and creating your own cycling adventure, preparing yourself for it is a perfect way to make it happen. Set a target, make it public, and commit yourself to being as ready for the test as you can.

You might think time is too short, your legs are too weak, or your spirit is unsure but, provided you're in reasonable health, you *can* get yourself ready for an awfully big adventure in as little as six weeks. I've done it twice, and I'm not getting any younger!

If you have longer, then great, but if you don't, then I'd say you just need to get on with it.

Age is no barrier, either, at least up to a point. I was nearly 52 when I did my first coast to coast ride – the longest ride I'd ever done to that point. I was nearly 54 when we rode over 900 miles from Paris to Venice and managed about 50,000 feet of climbing in two weeks.

I planned to do it again (or something equivalent) for my 60th birthday. In fact, we 'only' managed a long weekend in the Pyrenees in 2016, but we made up for it with another epic trip in 2017.

In the intervening years, various combinations of the group fitted in all kinds of rides, although I was disappointed to miss out on John O'Groats to Land's end in 2013.

In fact, loads of cyclists carry on well into their sixties, seventies or later, so I'm far from unusual (and certainly not exceptional!). I am lucky enough to be blessed with good health (so I am able to increase my training and so get myself fitter) but I've never been naturally strong or even especially energetic.

One thing I read (and have repeated often, so it must be true), is that every hour you spend cycling adds, on average, about an hour to your life expectancy. In other words, cycling time is completely free time. And not just time, but pleasure, adventure and a sense of wellbeing, for all the time you're on the bike and for some time afterwards.

All free!

Given the improvements to your health and quality of life that cycling fitness will bring you, it's no surprise that cycling is one of the world's fastest-growing leisure activities.

So, now you have a better excuse than ever to make the time, beg the time or simply take the time to get on your bike and ride yourself to fitness and a longer life. The choice is yours, and that adventure of a lifetime (or as many of them as you can fit in) is yours for the taking.

Table of Contents

Contents

- Cycle Touring for Beginners 1
- You Really Can Become a Cycle Tourist in Six Weeks or Less 2
- Feeling the Urge 7
- The Machine You Rode in On 9
  - Road Bikes 11
  - Real Tourers 12
  - Mountain Bikes 13
  - Hybrids 13
  - Cyclocross, Adventure and Gravel Bikes 14
  - Conclusion 15
- Training for Your Target Mileage 17
- Do the Splits! 20
- Spinning 22
- Carry that Load 25
- Make Time 29
- Building Your Stamina 30
- Fuelling Your Body 33
- Look Ahead and Start Gathering Kit 39
- Stay Focused by Looking Ahead 43
- I Found a Shortcut! 46
- Transporting Your Bike 48
- Rough Weather Riding 51
- Time To Dream 53
- How Hard Should You Train? 56
- Plan a Training Camp 58

The Nitty-Gritty 60

Your Long Rides 62

Avoid Tiring and Tiresome Trouble With Tyres 65

Become a Better Rider 69

Get Off Your Bike 71

Staying in the Saddle 74

Gearing Up 77

Staying Alive 81

Route Planning 84

A Change is (almost) as Good as a Rest 87

Practise Climbing 89

Touring on a Budget 91

Navigating Towns and Cities 96

Surviving Your Long Ride 98

What Doesn't Kill You Makes You Stronger 102

Latest Findings 104

Appendix 1 – Training Schedule 107

Appendix 2 – Tools and Spares 108

Feeling the Urge

The first day of March is, by some people's reckoning, also the first day of spring. Although the air can still feel pretty nippy, we can be fairly sure by then that it will soon be warm enough for even fair-weather cyclists to venture forth.

So, our thoughts are turning towards long summer rides, weekend tours and maybe even a bigger expedition. If you're anything like me, though, every winter seems to give me enough excuses not to ride, so every year I arrive at spring suffering from a severe lack of miles. My early season rides are always abysmal! And yet, come the summer, I can be riding centuries, through the night rides and even longer tours in the hills and mountains.

If I can do it, you probably can too.

On each of those abysmal early season rides I remind myself I'll be stronger tomorrow, and I always am. And we'll all be stronger come the warmer weather for every mile we ride now, so let's get to it.

This book is not for racers. If you're not into racing, but you think long day rides and touring might be more your thing, this book will help you prepare for the challenges that lie ahead. The advice is based on personal experience gained in the lead up to our Paris-Venice adventure in 2010 and during the trip itself, my St Malo-Paris-Lourdes trip in 2017, and many other long rides and training sessions, with a few words of wisdom from professionals and other experts.

You might not be crossing the Alps or hitting the Pyrenees, as we did, but if you're adventurous you will have to face hills and other tests that might well be too much for you right now. I think climbing the Timmelsjoch, where we crossed the Alps from Austria to Italy in 2010, Le Tourmalet (2016) or the Col d'Aubisque (2017) would probably kill me if I tried them without training, but I managed all of them in due course, and I haven't finished yet.

The key is training. The more the better, but you can do more than you imagine in the time you have available.

So, go on – amaze yourself.

The Machine You Rode in On

Riding almost any bike is better than not riding a bike, so I'm not going to give you the excuse not to ride until you get the right one for you. However, the sooner you start riding the bike you'll be using for your big ride or tour, the better.

So, one thing to consider early on is the machine you'll be spending all those hours so intimately connected to. You might soon be cursing it if you choose the wrong one or don't set it up properly, so let's address that first of all.

A few years ago, any experienced cycle tourist or bike shop expert would have pointed you towards a purebred touring bike for 'serious' touring. I was looking for one myself when I first started cycle touring, and eventually bought a classic Dawes Super Galaxy just in time to use it for our 2017 trip.

So, I still think they offer the best compromise between speed, comfort and luggage carrying capacity, and I truly love my 'new' bike, but I managed perfectly well on an old mountain bike for most of the previous ten years. I had a new hybrid bike for a short time (which also would have been ok), before I traded it in against the Dawes.

In fact, I seem to have against current trends, as we increasingly see people touring on mountain bikes, and hybrids, as well as multi-purpose bikes and 'tourers' that are somewhere between the traditional tourer and a mountain bike. A sturdy, comfortable frame, bulletproof wheels, fatter tyres and mounts for racks and bottles, mean these tourers are happy to carry you on gravel tracks and terrible roads, on the flat or in the mountains. These are built for marathon rides and world tours. You probably don't need anything that sturdy (or expensive), but it's an option.

Another alternative is a cyclocross bike like the Specialized Tri Cross (no longer available new but a fine bike if you find one).

There are three things to consider above all when you're choosing a bike for your tour:

1. Comfort – will you want to ride this bike for four, six, ten hours a day, day after day?
2. Capacity – can it carry, or be adapted to carry, enough kit safely and securely?
3. Construction – probably most important is the question, "Is it up to the job?"

When you add a full complement of touring kit to your bike you'll be adding a lot of weight – probably at least doubling the weight of the bike and probably more.

Bikes of all types can be built from steel or aluminium alloy. In general, I would still say carbon-fibre bikes are not suitable for heavy loads, unless you're planning a very lightweight tour. Titanium can also be used, although it's very expensive. In general, steel bikes are more forgiving and will give a more comfortable ride, while alloy frames are more rigid, usually lighter, but more liable to transmit shock and vibration to the rider. Some alloy-framed bikes have special features like frame inserts and many have carbon forks, to compensate for this, so that alloy bikes in general are now more common than steel.

Two recent developments (since this book was first published) are gravel bikes and a trend towards more relaxed road bikes. Many of these are carbon, as many again are aluminium (usually cheaper) and a very few are steel. Because they have the capacity for wider tyres (especially gravel bikes), they can be suitable for touring. In fact, you can tour on anything, but the better your equipment the more likely you are to enjoy the experience and come back for more.

Disc brakes are becoming the default for many manufacturers and the technology is now well-sorted and relatively inexpensive. Discs have definite advantages in bad weather, as the discs stay cleaner and drier, and discs are generally more powerful anyway. Hydraulic discs are more powerful and 'modulated' than mechanical ones, on the whole. Good brakes are an even bigger plus when you're heavily loaded for a tour.

With discs, the rims can be made a more optimal shape and they won't get worn away by the brakes, so should last longer.

Road Bikes

A lightweight road (racing) machine isn't built to take the kind of weight you'll be carrying as a tourist. Wheel rims, hubs, spokes and even tyres won't be up to it, even assuming you can attach the carriers you'll need to fix your panniers to. It's likely the frame won't last too long, either.

Of course, a road bike is okay for a day ride, but as soon as you need to carry any significant luggage at all, you'll be looking for something different.

A 'supported' tour, where a vehicle is used to transport all your luggage, can be done on a road bike, as long as you can carry, or have access to, enough food and water to keep you going. In that, you are basically doing what a Tour De France rider does, but presumably a lot slower. Spending day after day on a fast road bike is not much fun, though, unless it's designed to be more 'relaxed' (see above).

Real Tourers

'Real' touring bikes have sturdier wheels, tyres and frames, plus proper lugs to attach luggage racks on the front and rear. Because they have 'drop' handlebars some people confuse them with road bikes, but they have a longer wheelbase and more relaxed geometry, which makes them more stable with a load, and more comfortable. Drop bars give you more options for your hand positions and being able to ride 'on the drops' means you can get into a more streamlined position and ride faster when conditions allow – or when you're battling a headwind.

With wide-ranging gears as well, the design of touring bikes has evolved over the years to make them the best option for loaded cycle touring.

The Dawes Galaxy is a classic touring bike

Mountain Bikes

Some mountain bikes are also able to take luggage racks (on the rear only), and they'll have sturdy frames and wheels to cope with off-road riding. They also tend to use fatter tyres, which can make riding more comfortable but also add a lot to drag and consequently will be slower. Straight bars mean you're sitting up all the time, also slowing you down a little. That's always been my excuse, anyway!

You can get relatively slick road tyres in mountain bike sizes – I used 26x1.5 road tyres and they made a big difference compared with fatter, knobbly off-road tyres. Mountain bikes tend to be shorter than tourers, which can limit the size of panniers they can carry without obstructing the pedals – I managed to kick the panniers off my bike a few times until I learned to mount them as far back as possible, so they just cleared my heels. Having a rear carrier only also means the weight of your luggage can make the bike very tail-heavy, to the point where the front wheel starts to leave the ground on climbs and handling gets tricky. But there are ways around this, including adding a bar bag.

Hybrids

Hybrid bikes tend to have frames somewhere between mountain bikes and tourers – often looking like lighter versions of mountain bikes. They'll have reasonably sturdy wheels to cope with mixed riding, including potholes, curbs and the occasional track. They're also aimed at commuters, which means they'll be equipped with carriers or at least have the lugs needed to attach them. Again, these will usually be on the rear. They often have straight bars, but there are variations that may allow you to stretch out into a more streamlined position as well. However, they may not have the range of gears you need in standard form, so watch out for this. Hybrids tend to be quite tall at the front, meaning you struggle to get into an aerodynamic position, which is very noticeable in headwinds. I owned a Specialized Sirrus for a while but replaced it with a Dawes Super Galaxy just before our 2017 trip.

The Specialized Sirrus is a typical hybrid bike

Cyclocross, Adventure and Gravel Bikes

The right cyclocross bike is possibly the most versatile bike of all. They give riders advantages of a strong frame built to cope with the off-road demands of cyclocross racing and light weight (again for speed). They usually have a longer wheelbase than road racing bikes, making them more comfortable on long rides, and 'drop' handlebars. They may also have the gearing you need. If they have mounts for attaching carriers (many do but not all), they can be converted into very good touring bikes. Two of the team on the Pyrenees trip and Paris to Venice used Specialized Tri-Cross cyclocross bikes (and I envied them!).

Gravel bikes and 'adventure' bikes, like the Ridgeback Ramble, are also tough, versatile and comfortable on long rides. The Ramble is designed as an adventure, touring or commuting bike, has fittings for racks and wide-ranging gears. It also has a steel frame with carbon fork, which makes it unusual, but most big manufacturers have an equivalent in their range.

The Ridgeback Ramble 2.0 'adventure/tourer'

Conclusion

Get the best bike you can but make sure it's sturdy rather than slick if you have to choose one quality over the other. My mountain bike is old, heavy and slow, but it got me to Venice, carrying all my kit, and I haven't broken anything on it - yet! It still has most of its original parts, including the original wheels (hubs, spokes and rims!). The only major part I've replaced is the rear derailleur, for under £20, and that was worn, not broken. If it hadn't been obsolete I could have repaired it.

Update, 2017 – I have now replaced the rear derailleur twice. Once for wear and again when the new one got tangled in the rear wheel. I also wore out the wheel rims (as I realised descending Le Tourmalet…), but not the hubs, and even the derailleur incident didn't break any spokes. The nearly new wheels I fitted are lighter and faster but I'll never know if they would have lasted as long because the bike is now retired from touring duties.

Try to acquire the bike you intend to use for your big ride as soon as possible so you can train on it and get used to every aspect of its character. This includes gearing, braking and handling, both unladen and laden. Getting your bike right away will also give you time to set the bike up to suit your proportions and riding style and set yourself up to ride it just as efficiently. Jumping on a strange bike that's even slightly different from the one you're used to can feel disorientating and might even cause you injury, especially under stressful conditions (eg, in the mountains) and with long hours in the saddle.

That said, there is something to be said for the 'ride it until it fits' idea. Your body adapts to the bike to some extent, which is why a different bike can give you problems.

But a bike fit is often a good idea to make sure your bike is as close to the optimum as possible. Quite small adjustments in saddle height, bar height and reach can have a significant effect on your performance, endurance and comfort.

Training for Your Target Mileage

I'll get to the hills later, but for now I want to deal with the issue of distance. If you're feeling daunted by the idea of riding hundreds of miles, or even tens of miles, let me reassure you that you will be able to steadily increase your range up to the distance you plan to ride on the day, or even day after day. And you can do so surprisingly quickly. A few miles will soon become five, then ten, twenty, thirty, and so on, in just a few weeks, as long as you persevere and don't push yourself too hard too soon.

So here I'm going to discuss your training miles and how they relate to your maximum range. You will find a training schedule in Appendix 1, but here I will explain my thinking on the subject of structured training.

You can approach training for your big ride in two ways: either you need to get to a certain length of training ride to prepare for a specific challenge - say a 'century' (100 miles) - or you can plan your ride or tour based on how much you've been able to train. You can and will get fitter during a long tour but it's best not to be dying in the saddle on day one!

A very good rule of thumb (according to me and many others) is that your maximum range for a one-day ride will be roughly three times your *average* training ride (not your longest!). That assumes you train a few times a week, so your fitness is at least maintained and more likely improved over time. So, if you regularly do thirty or so miles, a century shouldn't be too much for you, especially if you've done a few fifty or sixty-mile rides in training. You will be tired by the end, but you should be able to make it. It's not just physical fitness that develops over time – you will also have learned enough by then to manage your resources to get you to the end.

For a longer tour you need to have something 'in the tank' at the end of each day so you can go again the next morning. I found sixty miles (about 100 km) was a realistic daily mileage on the tour (with all our kit, remember), but this came down to about forty miles on a couple of big climbing days. This was based on training mileage around thirty to forty miles per ride, with a few bigger rides, plus weekends spent in the Yorkshire Dales to get some climbing practice.

So, base your maximum range on three times your training average for a one-off ride, and maybe twice your training rides for a multi-day tour. Of course, the more training you can do, especially loaded and in hilly terrain, the stronger you will be. I got by on Paris-Venice, but I was the slowest and weakest, especially at first and on the longer climbs. I blamed the heavy bike and my age, but more training would certainly have helped.

By 2017, I had a better bike, and 'warmed up' by riding from St Malo to Paris on my own (so probably more slowly) before I met the rest of the team for the main trip. That was three fairly long, steady days on my own, but with no mountains. It was also a wonderful little adventure, my first solo tour, and unsupported. I loved it!

You should build your mileage gradually, but you can expect to be comfortably (comfort being a relative term) up to scratch within six to eight weeks. Training in weeks seven and eight can then be basically similar to week six, perhaps with more weight added to the bike. After that, more cycling will help you improve your strength, technique and speed, all of which will come with practice.

But, really, you'll be ready to go, and you could take on a century or a longer tour after just six weeks of reasonably structured training.

As I said, you'll find a helpful training schedule in appendix 1.

Do the Splits!

No, I don't mean for you to get into extreme gymnastics. Although flexibility is important, and cycling can have an adverse effect on flexibility, you don't need to go quite that far.

The 'splits' I'm talking about are the kind you measure with a stopwatch or, in this case, a cycle computer or wristwatch. You can divide your ride into as many arbitrary parts as you like, but the most important split is between the first half and the second half of your ride.

On a moderate ride - say around 10-20 miles - it will be quite natural to do a 'negative split', which means you'll probably do the second half quicker than the first (except, perhaps, the first few times you do that distance). This is because it takes a few miles to warm up and get into your rhythm, and then it's very tempting to push hard towards the end of a ride if you're still feeling strong. The difference between the two halves can easily be five minutes or more.

On a longer ride, though, you will find you feel strongest long before half way, and it's easy to go out too fast because you feel so good, only to suffer at the end. Many a strong rider has 'bonked' or 'crashed' (meaning, completely run out of energy) before the end of a long ride, when they felt great for most of it and were really flying at half way.

So, try to ride within yourself for the first half of a ride, even if you know you could go faster, so you do a negative split over the longer distances too. It's not always easy to hold back, but it will pay you dividends.

Bonking is not fun, and you might just crash for real. Just one or two miles per hour less can be enough to save a significant amount of energy - enough to get you to the finish feeling really alive rather than half dead!

Occasionally, in training, you will want to push yourself really hard, but in my opinion, it should be the exception rather than the rule, and definitely so at first. Training hard makes you stronger, but it can also be too much for you if you're not used to it.

'Bonking' affects you mentally as well as physically, and it can lead to dangerous mistakes and misjudgements, so do take extra care when you're feeling tired.

You'll naturally get fitter, faster and stronger over the six weeks or so. Listen to your body and be sure to rest after every big effort.

Spinning

Now I want to talk about the rate at which you turn the pedals, usually known as your 'cadence', which can have a tremendous effect on your efficiency, as well as the state of your knees.

You might be surprised how fast you need to spin the pedals, especially if you haven't ridden for a long time, and the optimum cadence is faster than most people find comfortable, at least to begin with. But there's a reason why you see Tour de France riders turning their pedals so fast, and it's not just because they're racing and going much faster than you - that difference is easily accounted for with different gearing.

No, the reason they pedal so fast is because it's more efficient, leaving them stronger at the end of a long stage and allowing them to do all that climbing without getting off and walking! Of course, they are much stronger and fitter than you and me, but so are all the riders they're competing against, so a kind of natural selection has honed their cycling technique to be as efficient as possible. Anyone doing it 'wrong' won't be able to keep up, however fit they are.

And when it comes down to it, these multi-stage racing cyclists are really just very fast tourists, covering a hundred miles or more per day, at maximum efficiency, so we can certainly all learn from them.

So, what is the optimum cadence? Around 70 to 90 rotations per minute, or just under a second for every turn of the pedals, will make your riding a lot more efficient. It will also save your knees (although you might ache at first), since you'll be applying a smaller force through each knee per pedal stroke (doing the same amount of work with more strokes).

In lay terms, power (which is what you need to propel the bike) is equal to the force applied multiplied by the speed at which it's delivered. In other words, smaller pedalling forces are cancelled out by pedalling faster in a lower gear.

A higher cadence also tends to improve your pedalling technique, by encouraging you to push the pedals round, rather than just pushing hard on the downstroke - what the professionals sometimes call 'pedalling squares'. This means you push forwards on each pedal when it's near the top of its cycle, then downwards, and then backwards as you get towards the lowest point. With practice this becomes a smoothly circular effort. You can even learn to pull up on the pedals when you're clipped in, although not everyone masters that, at least consciously.

There is something to be said for 'cruising' in a higher gear and lower cadence when on the flat or a downhill, since you don't need much power then. I certainly tend to do this, especially when I'm 'draughting', which means I'm taking advantage of another rider's slipstream to have an easier ride. But for efficient riding when solo or when you're at the front and need to produce sustained power, you should keep your cadence high. Practise using your gears, change down just before you really need to on each ascent, and your cadence won't drop so much, and you won't be straining to turn the pedals and possibly hurting your knees.

For your training rides, once you've warmed up, you

can mix up lower cadence sessions to develop power (by riding less efficiently), with high cadence sessions to increase your leg speed and improve your technique.

Carry that Load

To state the obvious: the big difference between everyday riding and cycle touring is the amount of luggage you need to carry, and this makes a big difference to your riding, especially if you don't load and secure it all carefully.

On the first trip I did, a two-day coast to coast ride (Whitehaven to Sunderland) I was able to carry everything I needed in a small rucksack that cost only £10 from Millets. I also borrowed a bike for the trip, as my brother-in-law's spare mountain bike was a lot lighter than my own. As a first-timer, I had no idea if I would even be able to complete the trip, so I wanted as much help as I could get.

That also meant I had no option when it came to carrying kit, as the borrowed bike didn't have a rack or any fixing points for one. As we only had one overnight stop and we weren't camping I could get away with using a small rucksack.

A borrowed bike and a cheap rucksack

But it's much better, especially if you have to carry more than the bare minimum, to let your bike carry the load. For the next coast to coast ride, where we did east to west and back again, I used my own bike and I'd added panniers. We still didn't camp, but we were away for three nights and this was a step up in terms of the amount of luggage and overall weight. A heavy rucksack would have been uncomfortable and unstable.

Trip #2 - the mascot didn't make it

Even so, a loaded bike is a different beast from an unladen one, and it was important for me to practise riding with a load before tackling an even bigger trip with even more gear. It will be important for you, too, so it's a very good idea to buy or borrow some panniers, if you don't have them already, and start doing some training rides with an increasing load.

We did a few more mini-expeditions, carrying a bit more kit each time, in the build up to our big trip, and I'd advise you to do the same if you have the time.

So my advice is to acquire at least some of the kit you'll be using on the trip itself, well before you need it (including the bike you'll be using), and gradually get yourself acclimatised to riding with the extra weight. Not only will you get to know your bike better and get used to using your gears, you will also find you get much stronger much more quickly - especially if you find a few hills.

But do use your gears (a lot!) to avoid injury, or you might not be going anywhere when the big day arrives.

There's no 'powering' up a hill when you have a heavy load, and even standing on the pedals is a different proposition, since the bike responds differently to your pedalling and steering inputs. Instead, you'll have to use the lower gears much more and maintain a higher cadence and you might even need to get off and push - although I, for one, hate being beaten by a hill, however slowly I have to go up it!

A smooth pedalling style – see the previous section – and the ability to spin, will help you make use of your lowest gears without wobbling and falling off.

All this means you'll need to get used to a lower average speed and a relatively sluggish bike. But you'll really feel the difference when you next ride it unladen, and you'll be amazed by your power, speed and prowess!

You will probably find, in the end, that your speed on the flat won't be much lower fully laden, especially as you'll be getting fitter all the time. You might even be a bit faster in a tail wind, although headwinds will have more effect, too.

But you will be bowling along before you know it – except up the hills!

Make Time

Some tips are so simple you could almost feel insulted that anyone thinks you need telling, but this one could make all the difference when it comes to getting enough training miles in, and it comes from experience.

One of the things that puts me off riding is a lack of time. Not just the time for the ride, which could still be worthwhile - an intensive 30 minutes, perhaps, rather than a stamina-building 30 miles - but the time to get ready. By the time I've found my cycling shorts and top, plus however many layers I need that day, filled a water bottle or two, grabbed some food, found my helmet and gloves, fitted the computer, and perhaps pumped up tyres and sprayed some lube on the chain... and then allowing time for a shower afterwards... I've run out of time to do the ride.

So, preparation the night before, or first thing in the morning if it's to be a lunchtime ride, can mean you get to ride when even the thought of getting ready might put you off.

Of course, you don't always need all your kit to go for a ride, especially a short one. As long as you have your road-worthy bike, your helmet, and trousers that won't get caught in the chain, you can ride. Thousands of commuters ride like this every day. Any ride is better than no ride, so make time, however you do it.

Or, in my case, stop finding excuses not to!

Building Your Stamina

The more cycling you do the stronger you will get, but to build stamina (mental and physical) this means increasing your mileage progressively over the weeks. Remember, we're looking at doing at least one big ride at the end of all this training, and maybe a longer tour with day after day of pretty big and testing rides.

Your training should include at least one longer ride each week, with a minimum of two shorter rides - one intensive and one more relaxed to recover from the long ride. If you can fit in another medium-length ride you will see the benefits from that as well. But initially, three rides a week will be enough.

What do I mean by a 'longer' ride? Well, to start with, that might not be very long at all, but very soon you will find that 30 miles is quite straightforward. Now, how quickly you increase this will depend to some extent on how long you have until the 'big day' or the start of your tour, but increasing the long ride by about five miles per week for the first few weeks, and more later, will be nicely progressive and shouldn't over-tax you.

Within six weeks you can be up to 60-plus miles for your long ride, with an average ride of over 30 miles, which is enough to get you across the finish line in a 100-miler. All those miles in your legs will also give you the stamina you will need to ride day after day on a tour.

Your shorter rides can still be short, but will naturally become easier for you and you can increase the intensity to make them more effective. Take in some hills if you can - even if it means riding up and down the same small hill lots of times. Your medium-length rides can also become longer each week, generally around half the distance of your long ride.

So you might start off riding 10, 15 and 20 miles in week one, and be up to about 10, 20, 15 and 30 miles a couple of weeks later, and so on. The week before the biggest ride you might do 20, 35, 30 and 60 miles. This will give you an average of 36.25 miles – just over a third of your target of 100 miles and over half your touring target of 60 miles a day.

If you have longer to prepare you can progress more gradually but personally I would look for an earlier event or adventure to make sure my training is really focused. For me, and I think for most people, having a target or deadline makes it much easier to focus on my training. You can then 'tick over' at roughly the same weekly mileage until the big day, and you'll be stronger for it.

Remember, if you'll be touring with a loaded bike, to gradually increase the amount of weight you carry on your training rides, especially as the big day approaches. Try to replicate the real thing at least a few times. We headed for the Yorkshire Dales to prepare for the Alps. Surprisingly, gradients in the Alps were easier, although the 'hills' last much longer, of course! It was still valuable training and experience, though, and the time together was a nice reward for the many miles we'd ridden alone, just building our fitness.

Unless you're a racer you won't need to do much in the final week before your big ride, but you'll probably find you want to – a lot of riders get restless legs after a couple of days off the bike, which can make it difficult to sleep, although this often passes after another day or so. You won't get 'unfit' in a week (except by the very highest standards of 'fitness') and you might well have lots of other things to do to prepare for your trip, so don't worry if time constraints stop you riding in that last week.

If you do ride in the last week, please take it easy and take care. The last thing you want now is damage to you or your bike that could stop your big adventure before it starts.

Fuelling Your Body

I have learned a lot more about nutrition and the effect it has on my performance, in the last few years, so this section has some significant updates for the 2018 second edition. I will use italics to emphasise these changes, while leaving the original text intact. Many outstanding cyclists still follow the kind of advice I outlined then and there is no doubt that it still works just fine for many riders. However, I have found I can ride further and stronger when I follow the new guidelines.

The change has come about after advice from my wife, who has studied the latest research on ketogenic diets and helped me find practical ways to apply these ideas to my riding.

However, I can't claim to be properly ketogenic. It's very difficult when touring to stick to a ketogenic diet, but by tending towards higher fat and lower carbs I have found my stamina has increased, and incidents of 'the bonk' (physical and mental) are much less frequent.

As you start to ride longer and further, something that might cause you confusion and alarm is your diet and the fuel you need to power your body. It's very easy, in fact, to think you're making less progress than you are because you're low on energy or you run out of steam on a ride. And you simply won't be able to do the long training rides you need if your body doesn't have the right fuel.

When you start to push your body to its limits you'll discover a lot about how your ability and energy levels vary from day to day and how what you eat and drink can make much more difference to your performance than you might expect.

In fact, when you first start, riding for much more than half an hour without eating can be quite disheartening, as your blood sugar falls and your strength seems to leave you. It can affect you mentally as well, so that your spirits dip along with your physical performance.

Even with more experience, this loss of strength during a ride can be quite alarming. Realistically, you can't become less fit during a ride, but it can certainly feel that way. Remember, low blood sugar affects your emotional state and judgement as much as it affects your muscles. You can modulate this effect to a significant extent, though, by becoming less reliant on carbs and protein for your energy.

Even when your fitness is improving and your stamina increasing, an hour is about as long as you should ride without taking on some food. On rides longer than this you should graze as you go, starting not more than forty minutes into the ride.

You will probably find you can go for longer than this once your fitness improves, by modifying your diet, and grazing may become much less important.

But there are a lot of misconceptions about what to eat and when. The familiar advice is to load up on 'carbs' before a big effort and a lot of people, me included, have made a point of topping up with a carb-rich snack just before a ride, and taking a variety of high-carb foods and drinks to consume en route.

I try to avoid the high carb snacks and am more likely to eat fatty or oily foods, if anything, before a training ride. Touring is a bit different…

Eating a high carb meal the evening before a ride does seem to make a difference, but the effect of high carb snacks is very short lived. Although you will notice a boost in your energy levels in the short term, this quickly falls away, leaving you craving more food very soon after starting – probably within half an hour. In other words, you got no further with the extra snack than if you'd eaten nothing. And, to compound that, in my experience the need for food at that point is more urgent and acute than if you hadn't eaten at all.

What happens is that you get a blood sugar boost from the snack, your body reacts by releasing insulin, which quickly lowers the blood sugar level again, and you sense a sudden and quite dramatic drop in energy, at a time when you actually need more than usual.

However, for a longer ride you should take on extra fuel, and you should eat at regular intervals during the ride, before you feel hungry. That won't be easy, but you'll realise the value of it when you get it wrong! One clue you should be aware of is when you start to *think* about food, even if you're not conscious of feeling hungry. And a sign you should have eaten already is when you start to notice the smaller hills or begin to feel anxious or 'stressed'.

The only cross words we had on the Paris to Venice trip were down to low blood sugar – it got quite primal at times – and the only 'moment' I had on Paris to Lourdes was at the end of a day that just went on a bit too long, when I knew I needed to eat at least half an hour before the finish. I was quite irrational for a couple of minutes until I was persuaded to eat a handful of dried fruit and nuts…

What you should eat, if anything, before a ride, is a high protein snack, with smaller amounts of fat and complex carbs. Take a similar mix with you for a longer ride when you'll need to top up.

Now I would say you should eat more fat and less protein to increase endurance. Although energy is less easily available from fat, there is more energy in a given mass of fat than the same mass of carbs or protein. Once your body starts to burn fat you'll find your 'reserves' of energy are much greater. Protein, though less problematic than sugars (carbs), still has a similar effect on blood sugar levels and insulin production/insensitivity.

A fully ketogenic diet means no carbs at all, but I haven't found this to be practical, and I've certainly eaten some very carbohydrate-rich meals on tours!

Good foods to eat before a ride include fish, cheese and eggs, beans and other protein sources with some fat and carbohydrates. Protein mixes are also useful, and these can be taken in one of your water bottles, too. In your pockets for the ride you can take bananas, fruit and nut mix and protein-rich energy bars. I've found pears are refreshing and seem to give a fairly slow release of energy, but bananas are excellent fuel and easy to eat. Most energy bars are too high in sugar and low in protein and fat but the best ones are good, if more expensive. Look for the 'high-protein' ones if you do go for these.

Peanuts and cashews are a good source of protein with a little fat, that you can graze on as you ride. One word of caution, though - it's easy to choke on dry nuts if you're working hard and short of breath. Better to stop for a minute or two and get your breath back first.

If I'm planning to stop on a longer ride I'll often take a few slices of wholemeal bread and some cheese, cheese slices or vacuum-packed fish, along with fruit and nuts and a few bananas. Peanut butter sandwiches can be good too. The best energy drinks do seem to make a worthwhile difference during long rides (as on the 114 mile Dunwich Dynamo) and I've resorted to them to fuel me for the last few miles of a big ride – a similar length charity ride I did on my own last year, when I was really struggling with ten miles to go.

Energy drinks can help in an emergency, not least because we need to make sure we are properly hydrated and pure water doesn't always do the trick if our electrolytes are out of balance.

Something I've also experimented with during a training ride is a protein shake, flavoured with coffee to make it more palatable. It seems to work, although I haven't used it on a very long ride.

Bullet-proof coffee is even better – add butter, coconut fat or whatever fat you find palatable to ordinary coffee. Coffee gives you a kick and the fat helps to sustain you.

If I stop at a shop for provisions on a longish ride I will often buy a pint (or 500ml) of full-fat milk, and drink that straight away. That's very often all I need for up to about 30 miles.

Other recommendations are flapjack – flapjack did wonders for me towards the end of the Dunwich Dynamo – plain biscuits, perhaps with chocolate spread, fig rolls and reduced sodium salt (to keep potassium levels high).

Some people recommend crisps, too, and milk chocolate is surprisingly good considering the high sugar content.

When you're really desperate, almost any food will do! But try not to get to this point.

Whatever you eat, always make sure you have enough water. Dehydration makes a big difference to performance and greatly increases the risk of cramp.

Something that's attracted a lot of attention in the last couple of years is beet juice. Tests have shown that endurance can be increased by up to 16 percent by drinking beet juice before a workout. This may be a result of nitrates turning into nitric oxide, which may reduce the oxygen cost of low-intensity exercise and enhance tolerance to high-intensity exercise. Some cyclists have reported very good results from drinking beet juice during a ride.

Pickle juice has become popular lately, but I haven't tried that yet.

Experiment with your diet to see what suits you and find out what you're able to eat on the move. You can experiment with a high carb snack if you wish but you'll probably notice very little benefit, if any, except on very short rides or training sessions.

But on days when riding seems like harder work than it should, or when you seem to run out of energy sooner than usual it will as likely as not be down to what you have or haven't eaten or drunk.

Look Ahead and Start Gathering Kit

If you're going to start carrying more weight as part of your training regime for a long tour you might as well look ahead to the tour itself and start accumulating the kit you'll be using.

The usual advice you'll get about cycling and touring equipment is to get the best kit you can afford, and I'm all for that. But what if you really can't afford much? Well, you can get everything you need (except a new bike) for under £100.

It will help if you have some basics to start with, of course, and your bike is going to be the most expensive item. I was lucky enough to have a mountain bike that was adequate for the job, and it's the one I used for the first nine years of cycle touring.

Apart from that, though I did need a tent, sleeping bag and mat, panniers and suitable clothes. If you have a suitable rack, your priority will be panniers. I found mine on eBay for the grand sum of about £17, including delivery, from SJ Cycles if I remember correctly, when preparing for our 2009 coast to coast trip. They're not the highest quality (and not fully waterproof, but that's what plastic bags are for) but they did a job for me and they're still in use in 2018.

Once you have panniers you can start to increase the weight you carry on your rides. Meanwhile, you can start to dream about the trip.

Other luggage can include front panniers (mine are small enough to use on the front as well), a top bag (to go on top of the rear carrier) and a bar bag. With no front rack, I didn't use front panniers (the other team members did). I didn't use a bar bag, either, for many years, but I bought myself one for our 2017 trip to the Pyrenees. It affects handling and steering but you soon get used to it. It also makes the bike more likely to fall over if it's not propped up carefully. Keep weight here to a minimum, but it's a useful place for smaller items and valuables, especially as it easily unclips so you can carry it with you when you leave the bike.

You can also get narrow but useful frame bags that fit in the angles between top tube and seat tube or behind the head tube.

On several trips I used the same small rucksack that I'd used on my very first trip, but as a top bag. That was a massive £10 from Millets and it is almost completely waterproof. I didn't put anything heavy in it – just my sleeping bag (in a bin liner just to be sure), some documents and a few snacks in the pockets– so tying it on with its own straps made it secure enough. Of course, I could have used bungee cords as well. Be careful with this if you try it and don't put anything heavy that high up on the bike, anyway.

For the 2017 trip to Paris and the Pyrenees, I retired the rucksack and used a plastic stuff sack that I'd got free from a charity event. Again, it was just the sleeping bag in there, with my documents and valuables being in my bar bag.

When we arrived in Paris in 2010 I realised just how tail-heavy my bike was. To improve this, I moved my small under-saddle toolbag to the front of the bike's top tube – tying it on with some fabric straps – so that the 'top bag' could be pulled forwards about six inches

(15cm). Being squashable meant it could be squeezed under the saddle and tied to the seat tube. This made a surprisingly big difference to the bike's stability. Now I use a bar bag (and my Dawes tourer has a longer wheelbase, which also helps), this tail-heaviness is not really an issue.

Now, you may or may not want to improvise as much as I did (and still do), but my point was to prove I could tour on a budget. I did buy a real tent, albeit a very small and budget-priced one, which cost me just £32 and which only weighs about 1.5kg. Cheap tents are easy to find, but cheap tents that are light enough, pack small enough and stay waterproof are another matter. I found a Gelert Solo tent on Amazon. It's not much bigger than a coffin but it did the job in 2010 and again in 2017

My sleeping mat cost less than £20, also from Amazon and I replaced it in 2017 with one that cost not much more. Clothing-wise, shop around and buy mainly polyester clothes that dry in minutes, are light and pack very small. Layering is important for changing weather conditions and a waterproof jacket (at least) is essential. I didn't bother with waterproof trousers – skin dries more quickly and it's very easy to overheat in long trousers, except in the coldest conditions.

We did get very wet a few times, but never too cold, and we soon dried off again.

Again, none of your clothing has to be very expensive. Padded cycling shorts or bib shorts can be pricey but there are budget priced ones as well that will last you a few weeks of a tour, at least. I've never bothered with bib shorts, and I've always been comfortable enough in the various padded shorts I've used over the years. They are quite a lot cheaper, too, if that's a factor for you. They are also much more convenient at toilet stops.

If your clothes wash and dry quickly you only need a few changes, and unless you're planning on fine dining, very few people will worry that your dress code always veers towards 'casual'.

Meanwhile, whatever kit you buy, start to ride your bike carrying some of it, gradually getting used to the kind of weight you'll be coping with and the changing handling characteristics of your bike.

Stay Focused by Looking Ahead

Training, and only training, can get tedious unless you can keep your goal in mind. This is especially true when you train alone and on the same routes time after time.

One way to stay interested is by timing yourself over your regular routes. You'll find you get stronger and generally faster, which is encouraging. Most people these days have a cycle computer to keep track, but you can just time yourself with a wrist watch or your phone. Occasionally, you'll find you're slower than last time, but that's okay, too. Conditions are rarely the same twice.

You can vary your route by riding it in the opposite direction. Better still, take a trip to a totally new area, and ride there. Think of this as a reward for all your hard work so far if you feel at all guilty.

Conditions change and we all have good days and not-so-good days. Each time you add weight to the bike you'll probably be a little slower, too. But overall you'll be making measurable progress, and any progress is encouraging.

But the focus of your training is the big event at the end of it, and planning that event in good time is not just important in terms of booking accommodation, transport, etc, but also for inspiring you to get out and ride when you don't always feel like it. A deadline is always an incentive, but we can easily kid ourselves that 'tomorrow will do' (or I can, anyway) or even that we might not do the tour anyway (especially if we're not ready).

However, planning the route, the transport and the accommodation does help to make the whole adventure more real, more imminent and more exciting. We can rekindle the enthusiasm that made us 'sign up' for the trip in the first place. Looking at pictures of the scenery, maps of the terrain and stories from people who've done similar trips before will all help to revive your spirits and get you onto your bike. If you can book some of it now you'll be even more committed – perhaps just the initial train, ferry, or whatever you need to get you to the start or home from the finish.

For a multi-day tour, most of us have a start and end date and an idea of where we'll ride from and to, or maybe a theme. One friend visited all the harbours around the coast of Britain. We aimed to follow the Orient Express across Europe for Paris to Venice, and lots of people do LEJOG (Land's End to John O'Groats). Our 2017 trip was designed to take in as much of the '100 Cols' route as possible, with the climax being the Col d'Aubisque.

Having a theme means you will usually be able plan a daily route and mileage and for a normal mortal (well, a well- trained mortal like you) your average daily mileage should be not more than about sixty miles. You'll have days when you feel you could have gone further and probably others when you'll wonder if you can make it to the day's destination. But we have always found that around 60-65 miles (about 100 km) is about right. That might sound like too much right now, but you can get there.

On hillier days (or mountainous ones!) this distance will be much lower, and probably around forty miles at most. While you might well be able to go further on flat days, remember that flat landscapes can be very exposed and a day of riding into the wind can be every bit as tough as a day riding up hills. Headwinds have much more effect on a loaded bike than they do on a road bike – all that luggage probably doubles the aerodynamic drag – and cross winds make controlling the bike harder work, too.

Tail winds are nice, though!

You may be an exceptional cyclist and your daily range could be more than sixty miles, but the aim should be to finish each day's ride by around late afternoon. That gives you a few hours' leeway if you're delayed or slower than expected. It also gives you time to rest, eat and recover for the next day's riding. In 2010, we often finished our days nearer 7.pm than we would have liked – leaving us short of daylight by mid-September, which wasn't ideal when we had our tents to put up and a meal to find. We were a little better by 2017, helped by having no mechanical issues at all, but there is always a chance you'll be delayed at some point. I had trouble finding my hotel for my last solo night before Paris, for example.

But the main thing for now is to start looking at those maps and get your juices flowing!

And then go for a ride

I Found a Shortcut!

No, this isn't the kind of shortcut that takes you further than planned and ends in the middle of nowhere.

This shortcut is ideal for you if you've either set yourself a very short deadline or you've fallen behind with your training, which amounts to the same thing. Alternatively, you might just not have the time to fit in all those hours on the bike.

It is possible to get fitter, faster. You'll have to work harder but it can be done.

Intensive training can help you build strength, but surprisingly it also improves stamina. By intensive, I mean the kind of intensity that hurts. Most riders spend most of their time near or below their lactate threshold. That's the level where you know you're working hard but you're pacing yourself so you also know you can sustain it for the length of your ride (energy permitting). Intensive training is sustained for much shorter spells, at your aerobic maximum (CO_2 max).

You can go to a gym or a professional trainer and do this very scientifically for the best results, but assuming you don't have the resources to do that, a simple solution is to get on your bike, find a hill around half a mile long, if possible, and (after warming up) ride up it as fast as you can in a low gear, spinning the pedals as fast as you can. Do this five to ten times, cruising slowly back down to get your breath back each time.

You can also do this on a flat road of about a mile, spinning the pedals as fast as you can. Use a gear maybe two ratios lower than you would normally ride that stretch, and don't ease up until the end. Ride back to the start in a much higher gear and lower cadence to recover, and then repeat. Don't stop to rest or you might stiffen up. Again, five to ten repeats will mean you've ridden a maximum of ten to twenty miles but with much more effect than if you'd ridden it at your normal pace.

You'll notice a big difference in your strength and stamina (and probably your cadence) the next time you do a 'normal' ride. It also makes an interesting change from just riding 'to get the miles in'.

You can add intensity (and fun) to your regular rides by attacking some of those hills with more gusto or just by including some sprints during the ride. In other words, forget about pacing yourself for today's distance and see how fast you can go, at least for short stretches during the ride. Allow yourself to finish the ride quite sedately if necessary, so your muscles get some time to recover before the end.

Naturally, you shouldn't be doing this intensive training, or any strenuous exercise, if your health isn't up to it. Speak to your doctor if you have any doubts and don't dive straight into the intensive stuff until you've done some easier riding and learned a bit about what your body is capable of.

Transporting Your Bike

Here's a tip that might save you some cash and heartbreak if you've bought or are buying a new bike, and/or you'll be flying or sending your bike on ahead.

If you need to send your bike via a courier or parcel service, or if you're flying abroad with it (or sometimes when you're taking the train) you will probably have to dismantle it and pack it into a secure parcel.

You can buy bike bags and boxes, but they vary in price and quality. Soft bags aren't suitable for air travel as they don't protect the bike from being crushed or bent, although they're fine if you're taking it by car or train. Rigid carriers are quite expensive.

So, don't destroy the box your new bike came in. If it was good enough the first time it will be ideal for you to use for your trip. Failing that, go to your local friendly bike shop and ask them to put aside one of their many boxes, along with some of the internal packaging. Bubble wrap is great and you can buy rolls of this if you can't acquire enough by other means.

Plan ahead with this, so you can be sure you'll have what you need when the time comes, rather than hoping to find a box at the last minute.

Oh, and you should practise dismantling and re-assembling your bike, too. That way you'll know what tools you'll need when you do it for real. You'll also be sure that none of the nuts and bolts are rusted or seized and that you'll know what you're doing when you have to do it on a station platform or airport concourse.

Take care when you reassemble your bike that everything is as it should be, and that your bike is safe to ride. I know from experience that it's very easy to forget to reconnect the brakes, for example!

I came back on the sleeper from Venice with my bike wrapped in about 50 metres of polythene dust sheet I'd bought from a DIY shop there. I had the bike in the compartment with me, so it was safe enough, but it certainly wasn't ideal!

It's a wrap! Ready for the train from Venice

In 2017, we had our bike bags delivered to our destination hotel, so we didn't have to carry them the whole way. Two were posted from home and two were ordered online and delivered to Lourdes. They all arrived safely, the hotel was happy to store them and we got our bikes home in one piece (well, several pieces that fitted back together!) by train to Paris.

All packed and waiting for the train from Lourdes

Posting essentials on ahead is a good way to avoid carrying things you won't need for the whole trip, and of course posting things home is a good way to lighten the load as you go.

Rough Weather Riding

Given the choice, most of us don't ride on days when the weather makes riding uncomfortable and cold, let alone dangerous, but we don't always get to choose.

Given that we sometimes have to ride in the wet and that a fine day's ride can often turn into a wet one, here are a few tips that might save you from a nasty surprise, a real scare, or worse.

First, the obvious point: wet roads are slippery, and they're much more slippery for a narrow bike tyre than for a wider, deep-treaded car tyre. Plus, on two wheels a small slip can mean a crash, rather than a minor adjustment, and you might be surprised how little grip you have when you most need it. Mountain bike tyres are better than road (racing) bike tyres in the wet, and touring tyres are somewhere in between, but you can still come unstuck all too easily.

Painted lines and road markings are lethal in the wet. On a fastish bend, drifting onto the white centre line can cause disaster. You basically have no choice but to go straight on, whatever might be coming the other way.

Wet drain covers and other metalwork are even worse - they're about as 'grippy' as ice. Previously dusty roads will also become greasy, and any oily patches turn into skating rinks.

Not only is cornering compromised in the wet, but so is braking. Your stopping distance will be much longer in an emergency, and the rear wheel is especially likely to 'let go'. If the front one does, you'll probably be off before you know about it. Braking on a bend obviously makes this much more likely to happen.

If you have conventional rim brakes, these will also be less effective when the rims are wet. This might stop you locking up so easily but it won't keep you safer if you just can't stop. The problem is worse in cold weather. If you have disc brakes these will still work almost as well as when dry, but that increases the chances of a skid.

So, when you have to ride in the wet, allow extra braking distance, keep your eyes looking ahead for potential slippery areas, like painted lines and other markings, drain covers and so on, and steer smoothly round them. Brake before you reach each bend so you won't have to do so mid-corner, and don't cut corners.

Take extreme care on descents. You may have almost no grip on a steep descent, even on a slightly damp surface, and especially from the rear tyre. Stay away from the kerb to avoid drain covers and debris, especially on blind bends and corners.

A loaded bike demands even more of its brakes and tyres. Although the extra weight might give you slightly more grip, you will also have more mass to control if you lose it.

For all these reasons, expect to ride more slowly in the wet and don't worry about it - allow extra time for a journey if you need to get there for a certain time, and don't expect to do a fast training ride, except on clear, straight stretches.

Time to Dream

If at any time you start to feel dispirited about your progress, it's time to look ahead again, and allow yourself to dream as you plan the tour and prepare a few essentials. Every little piece of preparation brings you closer to the goal and makes the big day more real. I like to do this kind of thing on a day when I haven't been able to train or training has been a struggle or when I'm otherwise a bit out of sorts.

If you're planning to tour in an area you've never visited before, and especially if it's overseas, getting hold of the best maps you can is priceless. It's surprising how useful a tourist map can be, in that it's designed for complete strangers to understand easily. There's no equivalent to Ordnance Survey in most countries, so 'official' maps you might buy will be less familiar than UK ones anyway. Foreign town centres can be really difficult to navigate (or escape from, as we found more than once) and tourist maps might well be the best bet for navigating these.

You can get maps from most tourist information offices, which exist in most towns and cities, at least in Europe and other developed countries. They may not have contours and so on, but they may have one-way systems, cycle routes and footpaths you can use. So, once you've decided roughly where you're going, contact the tourist offices in that area and request any maps and guides they can send you.

You can also find a lot of tourist offices have maps and guides on their websites, to print off at home. Only print the ones you need to take with you. Save them to your tablet, too, if you'll be taking that with you.

It's worth getting as many maps as you can well ahead of time, so you can learn to read them, pick the ones you'll take with you, and find key features like camp sites, hostels, busy places you want to avoid and quiet lanes you want to make use of. The more information you have, the better.

Two more things to sort out if you're travelling abroad, and you should do these in good time, too. One is your passport, which should be valid for at least six months beyond the end of your trip. If not, renew it in good time, especially if the peak holiday season is approaching. The second thing is travel insurance, which you may also need if you go to a country without 'reciprocal arrangements'.

Wherever you're going, unless you'll be starting and finishing at your front door, you probably need to book train, coach or air travel. Again, book early.

But whatever arrangements you need to make, look ahead, plan and dream. Talk about it with your fellow adventurers and let yourself get excited. Planning and dreaming is a great way to lift your mood, and it helps you make real progress towards your goal.

The Alps are calling…

How Hard Should You Train?

To get fitter you need to train, and to become very fit you will need to train hard, but training hard puts a lot of strain on your body. Overdo it and you can hurt yourself or at least exhaust yourself so that training becomes impossible.

That's why hard training needs to interspersed with...what, exactly?

Conventional wisdom says you should do at least two 'recovery rides' each week. These are gentle rides where you don't push your heartbeat too high or work too hard. There's no doubt that a short recovery ride helps to ease stiff muscles, and it might you help in that way. But a problem I and many people have is that it's difficult to make the ride gentle enough to make it a recovery session rather than just more training. Walking or gentle jogging is probably just as good - or a few stretches or even doing nothing at all...

In my experience, recovery rides can be either more riding than you need, since they don't contribute anything to your fitness, or they are counter-productive and add to your general fatigue. They also take up time when you could be doing something more useful.

So, if you're doing the required mileage and/or the shortcut training sessions to get you in shape in time, I wouldn't bother doing recovery rides at all. It's vital that you rest properly between heavy training sessions, especially after your long rides, while you build your fitness.

When you rest properly is when your muscles get a

chance to repair themselves and become stronger, and when your body gets to replenish its energy reserves. Any minor strains (maybe unnoticed) also have a chance to mend when you rest. This means that rest is as important to your fitness as all the miles you'll do in training.

So, do the training, but also take time to rest. You're not missing anything when you do!

Plan a Training Camp

So far, we've been focused on getting you ready for your big ride as quickly as possible, but you might have months to get ready, and something much more ambitious planned, in which case you can be following roughly the 'schedule' we followed as we prepared for Paris to Venice in 2010.

The winter of 2010 seemed long and icy, and most of us didn't get back on our bikes until well into the year. However, the tour wasn't happening until September, so we had plenty of time to get some big mileages under our belts...

You might be in the same situation, in which case the big day might seem like it's a long way off, but those months can fly by and leave you under-cooked if you haven't committed to a training schedule. Staying focused on your own for all that time can be difficult. It's a good idea to join your local cycling club and take part in their regular club runs, but getting yourself ready for a tour requires other preparation, too.

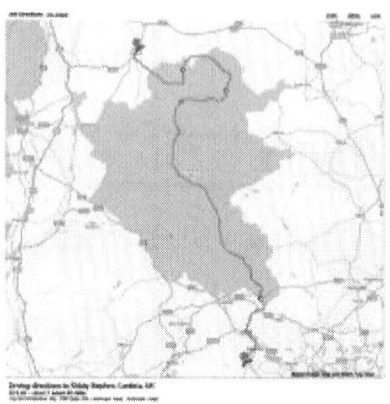

A weekend in the Dales

Our solution was to plan at least a couple of big weekends in demanding (ie, hilly) terrain. That meant that not only did we get those tough miles in, but we also had an extra incentive to train for the weekends themselves - which were mini tours in their own right.

I suggest you should do the same.

If you know you're going to be riding a loaded bike in the Yorkshire Dales, you have a very strong incentive to make sure you're as ready as you can be. Nothing quite prepares you for all that weight and an occasional twenty-five percent climb, but not to prepare at all would be silly. Two days of this kind of riding, of around 70 to 80 miles each day, staying overnight in hostels, or camping, is an intense experience all its own.

And those steep Yorkshire hills were very good, if intense, preparation for the gentler, but much longer climbs we expected, and found, in the Alps. But even without the big tour to plan for, those weekends were an adventure that made our 'training' fun.

If your tour is a long way off you will probably find you need some of that fun to keep you focused, so start planning a big weekend.

I wasn't able to join the others before the 2017 trip, so I had to be much more disciplined with my solo training. I didn't find a cycling club that suited my needs, either. I had to trust to experience and have faith in my preparations in little Jersey (nine miles by five, or thereabouts) to get me ready for a trip of around a thousand miles.

I made it, and you can too, but I advise you to make your training as interesting and adventurous as you can if you want to stay motivated.

The Nitty-Gritty

If you've been riding during the winter, spring or autumn - or off-road at any time of year - chances are your bike will have got very dirty at times. But mud isn't just a cosmetic issue.

A bicycle is basically a very simple machine, with some of its most important moving parts completely exposed to the elements. That makes routine maintenance quite easy, even for a novice, but it also means that those moving parts quickly get dirty, are stripped of their lubrication and start to wear.

So, every time you get back from a ride on anything but bone-dry roads, your bike will need a clean, especially the chain, chain rings, 'block' (that's the sprockets attached to the back wheel) and the derailleurs.

You'll also find your wheels get very dirty, and brake blocks get 'gritty', too, which wears the rims quickly.

You can use a hose or pressure washer on most parts of your bike, as long as you avoid spraying the hubs, steerer and bottom bracket – you could flush away the grease that they rely on for lubrication. Do will probably do more harm than good as a result, unless you are planning to strip them down and apply new grease.

In fact, it's a good idea to remove the wheels so you can clean all the nooks and crannies, especially around the brake mountings, fork ends and 'drop outs' (the slots that the whccls fit into). Take care with the bottom of the steerer, though, where the bottom headset bearing sits. This may be enclosed but very often it is open at the bottom.

Otherwise, a soft brush or sponge and a bucket of water with a measure of car shampoo will get rid of most of the grime. Specialist bike cleaners are better for getting rid of the more stubborn grime. Use a stiffer brush on the chain wheels and block. (Hint -a plastic toilet brush is ideal for this.)

For the chain, a proprietary chain cleaner is a good idea, or use the brush. Another tip I've seen is to tape two toothbrushes together, bristle sides inwards, so that the chain can run between them. Use stiff brushes for best results. You're likely to spray an oily, gritty residue in all directions when you clean the chain, so cover up anything you want to keep clean, including your wheels and braking services.

Rinse your bike with clean water, then dry everything thoroughly before lubricating the chain, derailleurs, brake mechanisms and cables.

For continued wet conditions and off-road riding use a thicker lubricant, especially on the chain, since thinner and 'dry' lubricants can quickly be washed off.

Your bike will last a lot longer, and keep performing like new for much longer, when you take good care of it. And that means more great miles and hours of cycling pleasure for you.

A bit of time spent on cleaning and maintenance is time well spent.

Your Long Rides

On a long ride you can, of course, expect to get tired. This fatigue can be both mental and physical, and the physical fatigue can have different causes and be felt in different ways.

Here are a few things you might experience, the probable causes, and what you can do about them.

Boredom, when you start to lose interest or enthusiasm while you're riding, is often the first sign of a drop in blood sugar. Very quickly, this can start to feel much worse – all kinds of negative feelings can surface and become almost overwhelming. You must eat or drink something at the first sign of this, before you reach such a low point. High energy foods or an energy drink are the quickest way to recover. A banana can have a transformative effect.

If you often get bored it could just be that you need to find a new route, ride with friends or take up a different sport to give you a change of scene or a fresh challenge.

If you feel physically weaker than usual during a ride this is also a sign of a lack of energy. Hills always seem steeper as your available energy falls. The cure (apart from increasing your fitness levels by training) is to eat properly and top up regularly on your ride if you need to. With experience you'll be able to anticipate this physical fatigue and eat or drink before you feel you need it. As you get fitter and stronger, the effects will be less of a problem anyway.

If you feel like rubbish at the start of a ride, and you

know it's not a lack of food, it could just be that you're developing or fighting a cold or other illness. Take it easy for a day or so and allow your body to recover or fight the infection. If the cause is over-training and fatigue, the same applies.

If muscles start to ache much more than usual, or to cramp, it could be that you're working harder than usual, but it's more likely to be simple dehydration. You shouldn't allow yourself to reach this state, but if you drink straight away and ease off a little, you can recover. Energy drinks with their electrolytes will help quickly, but water is fine, too, especially when you eat a mixture of sweet and savoury food at the same time.

Some people seem more prone to cramp than others and all kinds of causes and remedies have been suggested. I don't suffer often, and rehydration plus easing off works for me, so I can't comment with authority on other remedies, but pickle juice, beet juice, tonic water and increasing calcium intake are among the most commonly recommended.

You can make your own rehydration formula (or energy drink) in advance by adding some salt and sugar at the rate of one teaspoon of salt and one tablespoon of granulated sugar to one pint of water. I've also used orange juice, diluted about 50:50 with water, plus a teaspoon of salt. Whatever you have, drink steadily rather than gulping down a whole bottle, and drink a little more a few minutes later and then regularly after that.

If you start to lose concentration, have difficulty focusing or feel unsteady on the bike, you are suffering from low blood sugar and possibly dehydration as well. It's important that you stop immediately and have something to eat and drink. Don't stuff yourself with food but eat a snack or the equivalent of a very small meal, at most. Drink enough to wash it down, then drink a bit more. You should feel comfortable after this, not bloated.

A dextrose tablet or energy gel will also help if you hit 'the wall'. Personally, I prefer 'real food', but these concentrated energy sources are more compact and easier to carry, so you might prefer to use them, or at least add them to the mix.

Within a few minutes you should feel more or less back to normal, but if you need more time, do take it. Ideally, try not to stop for more than ten minutes, or your muscles will start to stiffen. I prefer to stand rather than sit down, to avoid the risk of cramp. If you do take longer, be sure to stretch carefully and take it easy when you re-start. Once on the move again, keep snacking and drinking at intervals to avoid getting into this state again.

All this depends on you having enough food and drink with you, of course. Try to never embark on a long ride without enough food, and especially drink, or without guaranteed rest and feeding stops en route. You might feel superhuman at the start of your ride, but you'll feel very different when you hit the wall with miles still to go.

Avoid Tiring and Tiresome Trouble With Tyres

Your tyres are a vital component in keeping you safe, keeping you mobile and keeping you interested.

Whatever kind of bike you ride, and whatever tyres you use, there are three things you need to do:

First, make sure your tyres are fully inflated (to the recommended pressure) before every ride. Check the pressures at least weekly. Soft tyres, even if they're a few percent below the optimum, make riding much harder work and this can be quite dispiriting if you're not aware of the problem. Use a track pump at home as they're much more efficient and will have a gauge attached.

Second, check the tyres' condition regularly. Perished tyres and worn treads will make punctures, splits or complete failure more likely. Don't wait until a tyre fails and causes you a major problem, miles from home or even puts you in danger.

Third, after each ride, and at rest stops during long rides, check the tyres for flints and other foreign objects. Flints can be as sharp as razor blades and can sometimes even get through kevlar-banded puncture resistant tyres. Thorns can do the same. Flints are more likely to be found after heavy rain (they get washed from fields and verges, or splashed from the gutter by other vehicles), and thorns, naturally, will be more common when hedges have recently been cut. You might also find nails and screws from time to time.

That said, a lot of modern tyres do seem much more puncture resistant than even the best ones of a generation ago. I'm tempting fate here, but I haven't had a puncture, except in very worn tyres, for a long time, even riding through broken glass on Paris cycle paths. In fact, none of us did. My Schwalbe Marathons don't even seem to wear, let alone get punctures

Tyres with the best puncture protection are also likely to be among the heaviest, but technology is moving ahead all the time.

Schwalbe Marathon with puncture protection

Always carry a spare inner tube and a puncture repair kit, including sturdy tyre levers (metal ones if you can get them), and a decent quality pump, as cheap ones don't last long. If your wheels aren't quick-release you might need tools to remove the wheel. It is possible to repair a tube with the wheel in place, assuming you can find the puncture, but it's very tricky, and replacing the tube is a much better option.

Also, always find the cause of the puncture (flint, thorn, etc) and remove it before re inflating the tyre. Run your fingers carefully around the inside of the tyre to find the cause of the problem. There may be more than one.

Tubeless tyres are becoming increasingly popular among road cyclists. They have been in use on mountain bikes for some time. They have the advantage of slightly lower weight and a greater resistance to 'pinch flats', also known as 'snake bites' (where the inner tube gets crushed by the rim in a sharp impact), especially at lower pressures.

This is especially good for off-road cycling, where lower pressures give more grip and a smoother ride, but there is also a trend towards slightly wider tyres for road bikes, which can also run at lower pressures with less effect on drag, and may run faster on rough surfaces. They are even said to be more aerodynamic when fitted to the right rims.

Tubeless tyres are becoming more common.

You will need tubeless-ready rims to fit tubeless tyres, though, and they can be difficult to work with out on the road. Getting the tyres to seat properly in the rims and give an airtight seal may need a track pump, at least. Again, technology is developing all the time, and some tyres and rims are easier to seat than others.

Once inflated, a special liquid, contained within the tubeless tyre, will seal most punctures very quickly – possibly before you even notice them, and allow you pump them back up to full pressure without needing to repair them at all.

Become a Better Rider

Apart from paying a qualified coach to improve your fitness and cycling technique, by far the best way to become a better cyclist is to ride with better cyclists.

Although riding with friends and family is a very pleasant way to get some fresh air and exercise, and any ride is better than none, this kind of leisurely riding is not likely to bring about massive improvements in your fitness or riding technique.

To get fit and ready for your big ride you should spend as much time as possible riding with strong, experienced riders. From experience, I can promise you will become a stronger and more able rider when you do.

For example, I like to ride with my brother-in-law, for two reasons:

1. He's a faster rider than me, as he's younger and stronger (mainly stronger). That means I ride faster than I would do solo, just to keep up with him, which of course means I should get fitter faster.

2. He has a higher cadence than me, which is something I know I need to improve, as many new or inexperienced riders do. I'm not conscious of trying to match his cadence but I know mine is higher when we ride together. As a result, my pedalling technique improves as well.

Riding with experienced riders we also improve other parts of our cycling technique, like cornering, riding in a group, timing gear shifts, and more. Again, we may not be conscious that we're learning these skills, but we are.

The biggest gain from all these improved skills (and fitness) is in cycling efficiency. Becoming a more efficient rider will be a big benefit when you're on your big ride or tour.

If you don't have an experienced cyclist friend (or group of friends) to learn from, I suggest you join your local cycling club and ride with them once a week - not just for fitness and to be sociable, but also to improve your skills and pick up advice based on their own experiences.

Get Off Your Bike

As a general rule, the more cycling you do the fitter you will get. And the harder you push when you're cycling, the faster your fitness gains will come.

But the problem with cycling (for most people, but to a varying extent), is that cycling mainly works on your legs, hips and bottom. Depending on your cycling position and style, as well as your physique and other activities, your torso and arms won't get the same benefits from riding, if that's all you do.

Some cyclists develop back pain, stiff or sore shoulders and neck, and problems with their arms, wrists and hands. These are mainly caused by over-use with under-mobility, and they're more likely to affect tall riders and those using road bikes. But it's a very good idea for all riders to do some exercise other than cycling, to strengthen the rest of your body and keep you flexible.

Core (torso) strength is especially important, for easing or avoiding back pain, and it will make you a noticeably more powerful rider (especially climbing and sprinting). You can find exercises online designed to strengthen your core muscles, including sit ups and various twisting and bending exercises. Yoga is said to be particularly good at building strength, as well as improving flexibility.

Body combat is another programme that brings big improvements in core strength (and general fitness), and it's fun as well, which makes it easier to stick at. Body pump is good too, and shadow boxing has a lot of fans, while weight training can be used to strengthen specific muscle groups. Five-a-side football worked well for me, too, especially on core and legs, and it's good aerobic exercise as well. Basketball is another you can try.

You can join a gym and take advice from experts on the best training for you, especially if you have existing health problems, but do make your training fun or you probably won't keep it up.

You can do some stretching exercises while you're riding your bike. Stretch your calves and achilles tendons during a ride by standing, with most of your weight on one pedal and pushing your heel towards the road for a few seconds, then change legs to stretch that one, too. Straighten your back from time to time by sitting up as tall as possible on a straight, quiet stretch of road, so that only your fingertips (or not even those) are on the handlebars. You can stretch your shoulders by riding one-handed. With the other arm, held as straight as possible, stretch backwards and then around your back. Hold this for a few seconds then do the same with the other arm.

Ease your neck by remembering to move your head! Tilt your head from side to side and also turn it from side to side, as well as up and down. Don't lose sight of the road unless it's completely straight and totally empty! Look online for videos of neck rolls and more neck and shoulder exercises.

Make a point of stretching during rest stops, too.

These stretches will help ease stiffness during a ride, but it's the extra work off the bike that will help most of all.

I should add that a stronger core and upper body (but especially core) will also improve your endurance, as staying in the saddle for hours will be less tiring.

There are other physical activities you can do that will strengthen your core while also achieving something useful. For example, I did a great job on my core muscles some years ago by spending most of a day using a strimmer to cut down an overgrown garden.

If you spend a lot of your time flopping in an armchair or sofa, the chances are your core is quite weak and you will soon flag when you're on the bike. Change that, and I guarantee you'll transform your cycling. It really is that simple, and strengthening your core is quite easy and quick to do.

Staying in the Saddle

After aching muscles, the most memorable after effect from most people's first bike ride is a sore backside. That's not such a problem if you don't need to ride again for a few days, but if you've got to get back on the bike tomorrow, or you're training regularly, saddle soreness can be a real problem. Some people are put off cycling for life by the discomfort of saddle soreness.

There are two types of saddle soreness. The first is a kind of bruising and tenderness of the 'sit bones' that comes from sitting on a fairly small seat for a prolonged period of time. You'll get used to this after a while, and adjusting your riding position, replacing your saddle or seatpost, or remembering to shift position from time to time will all help.

The biggest boon to a comfortable posterior, though, is a padded bottom or, more accurately, padded shorts. I managed without them for a long time but gave in and bought my first pair before I did my first 'century'. It's fair to say I was more comfortable at the end of that 100 miles than I had been on any of my medium length training rides without padding. Almost any padded shorts are better than nothing, although better quality ones will last longer and keep their cushioning effect for longer. You soon get used to the feeling that you're wearing a nappy, and most cyclists wear them, so don't be embarrassed.

The second type of saddle soreness is chafing, which is almost inevitable, especially in hot weather, although you'll always be likely to sweat when you work hard. This chafing can make your nether regions, the tops of your thighs and your backside very sore. You must take this kind of saddle soreness seriously, using antiseptic cream or ointment if it becomes infected.

But to avoid infection (and most of the chafing), use a 'chamois' cream or other kind of moisture-resistant skin cream. Personally, I have always used Sudocrem nappy cream, which lubricates, waterproofs and is an antiseptic. It lasts for hours between applications, and it's quite cheap, so I can use it liberally. Another popular and even cheaper alternative is vaseline. There are lots of proprietary 'chamois' creams on the market, and all have their advocates. Prices vary a lot, too.

A tip I have never seen elsewhere (so I'm almost embarrassed to share it) is to wear a layer *inside* your padded shorts or bib shorts. No one else seems to do this, but I find that wearing poly-cotton trunks under my padded shorts not only adds a tiny bit of extra cushioning, it also reduces chafing (by almost eliminating friction against my skin) every bit as much as using a cream. In fact, I don't think I've ever been saddle sore when I've done this. It does mean extra laundry after every ride, though, which might be inconvenient on a tour.

Talking of laundry, the other key to avoiding infection is cleanliness. Naturally, you should wash or shower thoroughly after each ride and dry yourself carefully - then apply some more cream if you are feeling sore. You should also wash and dry your cycling shorts carefully, too. Wash them with ordinary soap and water. (Detergent can be an irritant.) To dry your shorts, lay them on a dry towel and roll the towel and shorts up together, before wringing it out as tightly as you can.

This takes most of the water out of the shorts, which should then be hung up to dry.

Always have at least two pairs of cycling shorts on a

tour so you never have to put on damp shorts.

By making your riding more comfortable you'll enjoy it a lot more. You'll be surprised at the difference it will make to your ability to ride long and hard.

Gearing Up

If you've never toured before, or you're heading for the mountains for the first time with a loaded bike, you might have a nasty shock when you encounter your first real hill.

While you can get away with a narrow range of gears on a lightweight road bike, and even slog up a stiff-ish climb, when you add some luggage, a heavier frame and hill after hill, you might find yourself walking more than pedalling. I don't know about you, but getting off and pushing breaks my heart!

One thing you can't do so easily on a loaded bike is stand on the pedals and work the bike from side to side - the extra weight and lower speed makes this more difficult than on a lighter bike. So you will need to learn to stay in the saddle most of the time on hills, and turn a much lower gear. However fit and strong you are, you will need gears to climb big, long hills (or even short, sharp ones with a loaded bike).

'Twiddling' a so-called 'granny gear' is something you'll have to get used to if you do any serious touring in hilly terrain. It can be frustrating at first, pedalling quickly and going so slowly, but it will usually get you to the top, while standing on the pedals in a higher gear probably won't, though it can get you short distance (around a steep hairpin, for instance) more quickly.

This is another good reason to develop a fast cadence, as spinning the pedals for an hour or two at a time will be difficult if you're not used to it. When the time comes you need to settle into a rhythm you can sustain, relax your upper body as much as possible, and just keep going...

(I took four hours to climb the Timmelsjoch in Austria, although I admit I wasn't spinning so fast by the time I reached the top!)

The gearing you need to look for is at least 1:1 or lower. This means the biggest sprocket (at the rear) is at least the same size as the smallest chainwheel (at the front), or a little bigger. For example, both could have 32 teeth, although chainwheels can be smaller and sprockets can be bigger.

To get the range of gears you need, with high enough gears for easier, faster riding as well, you traditionally have always needed a triple chainset (three chainwheels) to go with your six, seven or eight sprockets on your touring bike. But rear blocks (the sprockets) have at least nine sprockets these days, and usually will have ten or eleven. And now, Campagnolo have just launched a 12-speed. So now you will often see only two chainwheels and a wider range of sprockets, as the gaps between gears will be smaller with more of them to cover the range of gears needed. On a purpose-built touring bike, a triple will be something like 30, 40 and 48 teeth, with a block from 14 to 32 teeth. Mountain bikes usually have a similar spread of gears, although the highest gears won't be quite so fast as on a touring bike and not many have triple chain sets these days. Some mountain bikes and gravel bikes have even gone back to single chainsets (known as 1x) with a massive range of gears on the rear.

I used my triple-equipped mountain bike unmodified on our tours until 2016 and it was certainly okay, if not ideal.

So, if you'll be using a bike other than a purpose-built tourer or a suitable mountain bike, make sure you have the gears for the job. Even some so-called tourers don't have the very low gears you might need in the mountains. Some people like to tour in the Low Countries, for example, and some bikes are built to do just that.

If you do need to modify your bike the cost could escalate to the point where finding a replacement bike becomes a better option.

For example: you can usually change a block (or individual sprockets) and one or more chainwheels easily enough. A problem might then come with the capacity of the bike's derailleur mechanisms when you try to significantly increase the range of gears in this way. Derailleurs can be replaced, too, but then you'll need to change gear levers (or more often combined gear/brake levers) to match, and so the cost adds up. You'll also need a new chain, although this is the cheapest part of the drive train and something you should replace quite often anyway.

But it is important to get your gearing right before your trip, rather than discover you got it wrong when you're already underway.

As your tour approaches, you should be doing a few rides with loaded panniers, etc, to get used to it. That should give you some idea of the need for gears, especially if you train in hilly terrain, but slightly steeper hills, much longer ones, or a heavier load, will make a surprisingly big difference on the tour itself.

Basically, you don't want to be straining on the bike - it's much better to be spinning.

Staying Alive

Although cycling can never be risk-free, it needn't be a particularly dangerous hobby either. If you're reading this you've no doubt come to the conclusion that the benefits of cycling easily outweigh the risks.

Even so, there are some simple things you can and should do to keep yourself and other road users as safe as possible. Remember, any accident you have will probably involve someone else as well...

The first thing you need to think about is visibility. On a bright, sunny day this won't usually be a problem (although even sunny days can have dark shadows under trees, bridges and in tunnels). It's a good idea to wear bright clothing whenever you ride, though, and fluorescent yellow or orange are the most visible colours you can wear. This is especially true on dull days and early and late in the day, when they visibly glow.

However, fluorescent clothing only works when there is some daylight to make it 'fluoresce' - it doesn't glow in the dark and it's not particularly reflective, either. So a fluorescent top is of no benefit before dawn or after dark unless it also has reflective panels or strips.

In low light, poor visibility and darkness, of course, you should be using lights, as well as reflective clothing and other kit. Most lights these days use super-bright LEDs, which have transformed the cycling world. LEDs produce a lot of light while using very little current, which means batteries now last much longer. They're also more reliable and durable than the older type with incandescent bulbs. Many LED light sets can easily last through an entire night-time ride on one set of batteries, and rechargeable sets are even better.

The best place for lights is around handlebar/saddle height. Mounting headlights lower down means they won't illuminate enough of the road ahead without dazzling other road users. Mount them on the bars and point them slightly downwards. Your rear light can be fixed to your seat tube, or rear carrier, but not too low.

Think about whether your luggage will obstruct your lights from any angle, front and rear, before you set off, and work out a way to overcome this, before you have to use them.

Flashing lights will make you even more visible and are now legal in most countries (and they'll last even longer in flashing mode), and there is nothing to stop you having two or more lights front and rear. There are lights you can attach to a cycle helmet, too.

On my last overnight ride, I used one good pair of rechargeable lights and two low-cost supplementary lights (costing a pound each....) in flashing mode. All four were still going strong when the sun came up next morning.

Night-time clothing will have highly-reflective strips or panels, using a similar technology to road signs, so they reflect light back towards its source (or to the driver of a vehicle) very efficiently. Panniers, bags and other equipment can also have these strips and panels, and your bike should have reflectors front and (especially) rear. The more reflectors you have the safer you will be.

Another good place for reflectors is your pedals. The up-and-down movement catches the eye of drivers, and reflectors on leggings and shoes have the same effect.

Of course, seeing and being seen is not much use if you ride dangerously, take silly risks and put yourself in danger. That applies even more when conditions are less than ideal. However visible you are on your bike you are still vulnerable against a tonne or more of car or forty tonnes of truck.

Statistics have shown that being highly visible does help to avoid collisions, but not nearly as much as you might expect. I would always recommend you make yourself as visible as possible, but I always assume that drivers might not have seen me, even so.

So, ride sensibly, especially in traffic, give clear signals in good time and try to make eye contact with drivers who may or may not have seen you at junctions, roundabouts and crossings.

Route Planning

I'm assuming at this point that you've been getting out on the bike and maybe spending some time in the gym or doing some other activity to steadily improve your fitness. If not, go back to the beginning, and get yourself back into the routine.

Meanwhile, it could be time to plan your tour in more detail. There are really just a couple of tips I would give you for this - start your tour easily and gently, and allow some leeway in your schedule.

By 'easily' I mean start with two or three fairly short days, with mileages below your maximum that will enable you to finish each day by mid afternoon (earlier in winter), so you'll have plenty of daylight and some energy to spare. Starting easily will allow you to acclimatise to touring and spend time in the saddle, probably with a heavier load than you've ever carried, without wearing yourself out. Your fitness will improve if you don't overdo it and do allow yourself enough time to recover at the end of each day's ride.

(We planned for the first few days of our Paris to Venice tour to be fairly easy, although we underestimated the time it would take to get out of Paris and we didn't anticipate the strong headwinds on days two and three. This meant the start wasn't as easy as I had hoped., but it did allow us to complete the planned mileages, despite the unexpected extra challenges. In 2017, I had three days fairly steady riding to Paris, at my own pace, to ease myself into the tour.)

By 'gently', I mean you shouldn't head for the hills and mountains straight away, assuming you have a choice. If you do have to start in the hills, then make the first few days' rides even shorter. Alternatively, allow an extra day for a leisurely ride before the tour proper. When my friends tackled the Pyrenees for the first time they arrived in Hendaye a day early and did a gentle ride on their day off before heading into the mountains the next day.

Breaking yourself in gently will allow you to check that all is well with you and your bike* before it becomes more critical or you have a tough schedule to meet. Feeling you could have done more is much better at this stage of your tour than feeling stressed about things from the start.

I don't always follow my own advice. On our last trip I found I had a problem with my brakes on my 'new' bike just a few hundred metres after leaving home, even though my brakes had been ok on several training rides. It took three or four days of riding with a front brake only before I found a bike shop that could help. Fortunately, this was before we reached the mountains!

Plan your route with a relatively gentle start and you should at least be on schedule for the first few days!

Include some leeway in your schedule by planning a rest day in the middle of a long tour or allowing a day at the end in case you're delayed en route. On Paris to Venice we took a chance by scheduling 13 days' riding without a rest day, but we did allow a spare 24 hours or so at the end of the ride, just in case. In 2017 we had a couple of shorter days at the end and then two days to ride in the Pyrenees from our base in Lourdes.

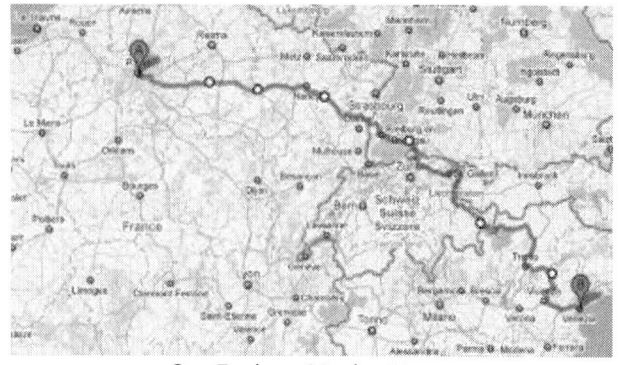

Our Paris to Venice Route

Planning a tour is exciting and it's tempting to be over-ambitious as a result. Resist - you can always do a few extra miles at the end of a day if you really want to, and you might need to do so anyway, to find shops, a camp site or an evening meal. On day one of Paris to Venice we had to ride an extra ten miles or so to the next town to get something to eat - then back again to the campsite.

Planning is fun but it's rarely perfect!

A Change is (almost) as Good as a Rest

One of the best ways to do something different, improve your overall fitness and develop your cycling skills is to go off road once in a while.

Borrow or hire a mountain bike if you don't have one, or put suitable tyres on the mountain bike you'll be using for your tour, and head for the woods and hills. Mountain biking gives you more of an all-body workout than road cycling, and a more intense training session in a shorter time, as well as improving your bike-handling skills. The change of scene will also add interest to your training, motivating you to work harder without really thinking about it.

But perhaps the most important thing is that it's fun.

You don't need an expensive mountain bike if you'll just be riding trails for a bit of fun, although front suspension (standard on almost all mountain bikes these days) does help to cushion the worst of the ruts and roots, protecting your wrists and arms from taking too much of a battering.

Hired bikes, especially at outdoor centres and mountain bike trails will usually be pretty good in my experience - and you don't have the cleaning and maintenance to worry about when you can just hand it back at the end of the day!

Tyres should also be run softer for off-road riding in general. This adds to the cushioning effect, allows the tyre to mould itself to the uneven surface and spreads the weight over a bigger contact area on soft mud or sand, which helps you stay on top of the ground rather than ploughing into it.

Wear a helmet and don't take silly risks but you'll be surprised what you're able to negotiate safely on a mountain bike with a bit of practice and with your growing skill and confidence.

You could be surprised how much fun it is, too!

Practise Climbing

If you're heading for the hills on your ride you probably already know it's going to hurt, at least some of the time. The thing about cycling for most of us is that it never actually stops hurting, unless we're riding with slower riders or taking it easy. Nothing wrong with that, but...

What usually happens as you get stronger is that you go faster, find steeper hills, carry more kit, or all three. Was in Bernard Hinault who said: "It doesn't get any easier, you just go faster"?

Well, on a tour, speed isn't everything, but I think most of us are inclined to push ourselves to go as fast as we reasonably can. Either that, or we head for the hills or maybe add more miles.

Anyway, back to the climbing. With a loaded bike and the right gears, and enough fitness training to keep going, the best technique for a long climb is to stay in the saddle and spin the pedals at about 80 rpm, or so. You will instinctively look for the highest gear that you can sustain that cadence in and, given a consistent gradient, that should be that until you get to the top.

However, you are likely to get stiff, possibly hot and probably a bit bored if the climb is very long, and it's unlikely to be the same gradient all the way to the top anyway. To break the monotony, get some air to your nether regions and cope with occasional steeper sections, stand for a few seconds - maybe 20-25 pedal strokes at a time. If the gradient lessens try going up a gear or two, stand up and do a short 'sprint' (these things are relative!) to avoid spinning uselessly in too low a gear. Then settle back into your saddle, your most efficient gear and your optimum cadence once again.

As you approach the top, and assuming you've got something in reserve, shift up a gear and accelerate over the top. Keep pushing hard, as the road levels off and you move through the gears. Often the most painful part of a hill is when we relax too much at the top, lose all our momentum and rhythm, and start to really feel our legs and lungs. So, unless you're stopping for a break or to wait for a team mate, it's often best to push on. In any case, try to ride on for a few hundred metres before you stop for a rest, if you need one.

Yes, climbing hurts, but it's a strangely satisfying form of suffering - and a great feeling when we reach the top. More than once, 'topping' a big climb has brought tears to my eyes – and not just from the pain and sweat!

Climbing in the saddlc (Pyrenees 2007)

Touring on a Budget

Cycling can be a wonderfully cheap way to see the world, and cycle touring has to be the best value way to visit new areas, countries and even continents - or just to explore the area around you.

If you're travelling a long way from home and you want to be self-sufficient, the price of equipment can still add up. There's no shortage of retailers and online stores willing to take your money, of course, but there are a few secrets it's wise to know in advance that will minimise the cost and make sure you have everything you need.

Firstly, start keeping your eyes open for useful kit as soon as you start to plan your tour and you'll be surprised what's available in off-season sales, closing-down sales, charity shops, from friends, second-hand or at bargain prices - even free. For example, any tough plastic bags, especially, resealable ones, will be very useful for your tour. We all need to cut down on plastics use, so any time you can re-use what you have, rather than buying new, you're helping the planet, just a little bit.

Panniers come in a variety of materials, shapes and sizes, as well as different levels of quality and price. Expensive ones will claim to be waterproof, while cheaper ones probably won't. The most economical approach is to assume that no panniers are fully waterproof, buy the cheapest ones that look sturdy and big enough, and wrap and pack your equipment, clothes, etc, accordingly. Use your polythene bags, especially 'ziplock' ones that can be sealed and resealed, for individual items. Some frozen food comes in resealable bags like this and they are often quite sturdy. If the appearance doesn't matter these are ideal, and they're free. Wash them out if necessary and collect them over the course of the weeks or months before your trip. It's not being mean, it's being environmentally aware…

Even carrier bags will do the job if they don't have air holes in them. Take a few spare bags and hang on to any that you acquire on the trip - they weigh next to nothing and take up very little space, but might make all the difference to your comfort.

Use a 'rubble sack' - a tough type of rubbish bag - in each pannier to make it waterproof as well. Simply fold the top over and tuck it in and your pannier will be as good as water-tight. A 'bag for life' from your local supermarket will also suffice. You can buy purpose-built liners but they're not necessary.

A top bag adds a lot of volume to your carrying capacity, although you shouldn't put too much weight this high on your bike. For my first trip, I used a cheap rucksack as a top bag, tied it securely with its own straps (you can use bungee cords as well for extra security), and stuffed my sleeping bag in it, wrapped in a bin liner for extra waterproofing. It stayed secure and dry for two weeks, including some very wet days.

In 2017, I retired the rucksack and used a stuff sack I had free from a charity event of some kind, this time secured with bungees.

We camped most nights on both trips, which is a lot cheaper than hotels or even hostels. Three one-man tents fitted on a standard sized pitch, so we often saved money there, as well.

I've already mentioned my tent (£32) and my sleeping mat (about £18). My first sleeping bag was one I already had that cost about £10 in a sale. I paid slightly more for a new one for 2017 but you don't need anything very special for a late summer tour. I've also mentioned my very cheap back-up lights and you can get a bright LED torch that will see you through a tour for a pound as well. There's no point spending more, in my opinion. Do get some good bike lights - the best you can afford - as your main set, but don't waste money on extras like a torch where a cheaper option will do.

Don't economise on safety, but do buy your spares and replacement parts when they're on special offer. You can often get inner tubes at half price, for example, and many other parts are discounted at various times. If you start looking early you can pick things up when they're at their cheapest, not at the last minute when you will probably have to pay full price.

A cheap pump may be a false economy. Although you can get enough air into a tyre to get you mobile, cheap pumps often won't give you the full pressure you really need, especially for a loaded bike. That will make for slow, heavy riding, and less than ideal grip and handling, as well as shorter tyre life. Cheap pumps also don't last very long. But shop around so you get the best pump you can within your budget.

It's worth paying more for good quality puncture-resistant tyres. Worn tyres can suddenly become very susceptible to punctures (even if they're puncture-resistant) as the rubber becomes thinner. Good tyres may also give you better grip and lower rolling resistance, although it's always a question of compromise, when set against durability and weight. You don't have to pay a lot, though. I bought two new Schwalbe Marathon tyres for £19.99 each.

Most tourists on 700c wheels will opt for 32 or 35 mm section tyres, while a good compromise on a 26 inch mountain bike wheel is a 1.5 or 1.75 inch road tyre. I bought Panaracer Crosstown tyres in 26x1.5 inch for my mountain bike and had no punctures on the tour (and very few afterwards). They're not reputed to be the fastest tyre but they are durable. They began to show signs of fatigue about three years later, and started getting punctures as the tread became very thin and started to crack. I replaced them with Continentals, which are lighter and faster but are also puncture resistant. The Schwalbe Marathons on my current bike have been faultless so far (and easier to fit than I was expecting).

Clothing is another area where you can spend a lot of money, or very little. Discount sports shops often have suitable clothes at a fraction of the price of the latest 'fashion' items. Most of them will be polyester, which is ideal as it washes and dries in minutes. I wore a cotton tee shirt as a base layer when required and nylon swimming shorts for modesty over my cycling shorts.

I also wore trainers rather than cycling shoes for many years, as I used toe clips rather than clipless pedals. I have 'proper' cycling shoes now, that I use with MTB-type pedals (a toe clip but no straps).

Any thick socks will do in my experience. You can waterproof your feet (and keep them a bit warmer) by putting plastic bags over your socks before putting on your shoes.

But the key to saving money on equipment is to keep your eyes open in the months before your trip so you can catch all the bargains. Also borrow and adapt equipment you already have, as long as it's not too bulky or heavy and doesn't compromise your safety.

Don't let a lack of funds stop you enjoying cycling to the full, because there's usually a low-cost solution. Cycling is about riding the bike, not posing for the cameras!

Navigating Towns and Cities

There has been a lot of progress in recent years towards making towns and cities more cycle-friendly, although some developments have not been so helpful.

For example, while dedicated and signposted cycle routes are a good thing, banning cyclists from the most direct route out of a city is not necessarily such a good idea. On Paris to Venice we wasted well over an hour escaping from the Italian town of Bolzano because the dedicated cycle route was closed for bridge repairs (although we could have walked it, we weren't allowed to), and we were barred from using the main road.

The biggest problem I had with navigating to Paris was finding the route out of towns where I'd either camped overnight or stopped for a break (or just couldn't avoid). That, and finding my hotel in Plaisir, near Paris. Between towns was easy, in comparison, since I could just head east...

The lesson from our Bolzano event, and others, is to not enter a town or city unless you need to, or unless you know for sure the route is easily navigable.

Most towns are not so unhelpful, though, and very often the best way to navigate a large town or city is to plunge straight through it, rather than following ring roads, bypasses or alternative routes. Even if you have to walk some sections, going all the way around a large town or city, often on or alongside unpleasantly busy highways, is not much fun and can add a lot of miles to your day's riding.

Generally speaking, though, unless you want to visit a particular place or you need shops or other facilities, I would advise you to always avoid large towns and cities by routing well away from them, rather than have to make the decision about going through or around one when you get to it.

If you do go through, follow the advised cycle routes but be prepared for pedestrians and their dogs, parked cars and other obstructions. Don't expect to travel fast, but by taking a direct route you should still save time and put yourself at less risk.

Surviving Your Long Ride

On a long ride you will get tired. That's almost the point of doing it, in my book - pushing yourself to go further, climb higher, be more self-sufficient - and survive the experience.

But to maximise the distance you can go, hills you can climb, and so on, you need to cut fatigue to a minimum, and decades of experience have taught cyclists how to do this.

The first step is to have your bike set up to suit your physique and proportions. Too big and you'll be stretching too much and be inefficient, too small and you'll be too cramped, and also inefficient. Inefficiency, of course, means you'll waste energy and become more tired than you need to be. You obviously need a bike with a frame that's roughly the right size for you, although the trend is towards slightly smaller frames than in the past, so that you can easily stand over the top tube (the 'crossbar') with both feet flat on the ground and a few centimetres between you and the tube.

This means seat posts tend to be longer than they used to be, as are handlebar stems. Adjust the saddle so your leg is still slightly bent at the bottom of the pedal stroke and you don't need to rock from side to side when pedalling fast. If the saddle is too low you will be less efficient (again) and your knees could suffer, too.

Your reach (the distance between the saddle and the handlebars) depends on the length of the top tube plus the length of the handlebar stem, and this stem can easily be changed on a modern bike. Stems can be anything from a centimetre or two to 15cm or more, so there's plenty of scope to get it right. Some are even adjustable and most can be flipped over to change the bars' height. Older quill-type stems (like the one on my Dawes) are harder to come by but easier to adjust for height.

Most people find that having the handlebars level with or a little below the saddle height is the best position for long rides. Although some people like to sit up straighter this is much less efficient, and unless you have a compelling reason for adopting it, like a bad back, I'd strongly advise you get used to a lower, more aerodynamic pose on the bike.

Once you have a comfortable riding position, there are a few more things you can do to stay comfortable and ride longer.

Inflate your tyres to within the recommended pressure range. Soft tyres make a massive difference to the effort you need to put in to ride at a given speed. I blame my slow progress up the Timmelsjoch Pass partly on low tyre pressures. I was always going to be slow but it was definitely harder work than it might have been. In wet weather you might compromise on this a little to give you more grip - you'll be riding more slowly anyway. Also, make sure your load is properly distributed so that balance and control are as easy as possible. Again, this saves your energy.

Wear good cycling gloves with adequate cushioning in the heel of the hand. This makes a surprising difference to the amount of shock transmitted through your hands, wrists and arms. In hot weather your gloves can be fingerless, while cold weather calls for more insulation and windproofing. Carry both so you can swap to full fingered gloves for long, chilly descents.

Shift your hand positions regularly. This isn't so easy with straight bars, but you can add bar ends to give you more options. Some are more comfortable than others. Take the opportunity every so often to rest your hands very lightly on the bars and sit up. This takes the weight of your hands and arms and allows you to straighten your back.

Relax your arms and shoulders as much as possible. Ride with your elbows slightly bent to cushion you from road shocks. Ride one handed from time to time and relax the other arm and hand by dropping it to your side and shaking it gently for a few seconds while flexing your fingers.

Stretch your legs and knees by standing on each pedal in turn for a few seconds (while coasting) and pushing your heel towards the road with your knee completely straight.

Staying warm in cold weather can consume a lot of energy - energy that you could use for pedalling...

Wear padded shorts for comfort and enough layers so that you don't feel chilled when riding (this is very draining after a while). Judging temperature can be difficult. As a guide, feeling slightly chilly at the start is okay, as long as you feel comfortable once you've warmed up. Wind chill adds to the chilling effect of cold air, so a windproof layer you can unzip to suit is ideal. You may also have zipped vents in cycling shorts, jackets and tops, and you can use these to help regulate your body temperature as you go.

A lot of cyclists get cold feet, even in warmish weather. I do myself, but it doesn't really bother me. In wet weather I might use polythene bags over my socks (inside my shoes) or you can use waterproof and insulated overshoes if you prefer.

To summarise: the best way to stay in the saddle for hours and cover big miles is to be relaxed and comfortable, as well as fit and well-fed.

If you're comfortable you can enjoy your cycling – and there's no point otherwise!

What Doesn't Kill You Makes You Stronger

Throughout this book we've been pursuing two conflicting aims: firstly, to get fit and strong enough to cope with a long ride or tour, mainly by working hard, and secondly, to learn to ride as efficiently as possible to make that ride or tour feasible and as easy and comfortable as possible.

We've acknowledged that the big ride will be a real challenge and I'll say again that in my opinion that's the whole point of doing it.

To become stronger we have to work hard, and the harder we can work the more strength we will gain. So it makes sense to work extra hard on at least some of our training rides, which makes them more intense and therefore shorter. Probably the best way to do this is to handicap ourselves. One way is to add luggage to the bike, which also gives us a chance to learn how it will feel on tour.

There's a simpler way to make riding harder work, though, which we can use more easily on a regular basis, or whenever it suits us, and that's to ride a heavier, slower bike on some of our training rides.

If you have a 'spare' mountain bike, fit it with the fattest, chunkiest tyres you can and run them at a lower pressure. If you plan to use your mountain bike for the tour (and your training rides) try to get hold of a spare pair of wheels so you don't have to keep changing the tyres - swapping wheels is much quicker. You don't need the best quality wheels or tyres for this - the point is to make riding harder work.

Personally, I acquired a cheap old mountain bike and fitted some fat tyres I salvaged from another scrapped bike. It's fun to ride, but it is much harder work than the bike I used regularly (with its road tyres). After one short ride on the road I could feel I'd had a harder, different kind of workout. Of course, when we go off-road it's be harder still.

Handicapping yourself in this way means you don't need to find a hill to build your strength. This might help you to avoid busy or dangerous roads as well, since you can get in a good, intensive workout almost anywhere.

Latest Findings

Quite a lot has changed in the eight years since we did Paris to Venice and even in the four years since I last updated this book we have seen some new developments in a variety of areas.

I have also learned more over that time. I have incorporated most of these changes and discoveries in the updated text, but one aspect wasn't covered at all in the first edition and another needs mentioning and expanding upon here.

Dietary research has changed the way I and many other people think about fuelling our bodies. The (UK) government's 'healthy eating' advice is out of date (although they are slowly shifting, without acknowledging they were ever wrong). Some will say they were in thrall to the major food manufacturers who needed a hungry market for their cheap and plentiful cereal (mainly wheat) based foods. The sugar industry has also been blamed. But the key is education and experience, and cyclists and other endurance athletes have discovered for themselves that a carb-rich diet is not necessarily the best way to get both fitter and healthier.

Research has undermined the assumption that cholesterol is always bad and therefore that low-fat diets are inevitably good. Not many things could be further from the truth.

So, my focus on fuelling for rides has turned away from extra carbs towards a higher-fat diet. Carbs can give an instant hit (and get you home or up the next hill) but they are useless for endurance unless you keep topping up. At least, that's my experience, and I've heard the scientific reasons why that should be.

Bike Fitting is less controversial, that's for sure, but very recently I've been reading about crank lengths and how at least fifty percent of riders are probably using cranks that are too long for them. (The crank is the 'arm' that your pedals are attached too.) Cranks that are too long can often cause problems in the hips, because we are asking our hip joints to work through too great a range. As was pointed out in the article I read, our hips have evolved to enable us to walk and run, and the large angles needed to pedal a big crank are outside the normal range of movements.

This is especially noticeable when we are stretched out into an aerodynamic position and our knees are coming up to almost meet our chest. If you feel comfortable with the pedal at the bottom of the stroke but uncomfortable when you're actually pedalling, especially on the drops, crank length could be your problem. I'll be experimenting with mine. If you do fit shorter cranks you should raise your saddle by the same amount, which will double the 'clearance' between your knees and chest. Leverage is reduced slightly with a shorter crank, but only by about four percent, studies show.

It will be easier to maintain a higher cadence with shorter cranks, so your total power output will probably be the same or higher. You are likely to be much more comfortable, too, and able to hold a more aerodynamic position for longer, which would increase your speed and could save you a lot of energy over a long ride.

And, after all, the long ride is the whole point of this book.

Enjoy!

Appendix 1 – Training Schedule

It's unlikely that you'll keep to this exact schedule – I didn't – but it does tell you roughly what you need to aim for to hit your target mileage in about six weeks, and how to get there. Think of it as guidance rather than rules and just try to make sure you do enough, one way or another.

Remember, you can always substitute a shorter, more intensive session for a longer ride, although your longest rides do need to increase progressively along the lines suggested.

Week	Miles 1	Miles 2	Miles 3	Miles 4	Notes and comments
1	8	10	10*	20	*optional
2	10	15	10*	25	*optional
3	10	20	15*	30	*optional
4	15	20	20*	35*	*add panniers and some luggage
5	15	25	20*	45*	*add panniers and some luggage
6	20	35*	30	60*	*add panniers and more luggage
7, 8, etc	20	35	30	60	with luggage on most rides

Have a quiet week before your big ride if you can.

If your ambitions are more modest (or more sensible!) you can do fewer training miles. It's your body and your life, so it's up to you how hard you push yourself.

Appendix 2 – Tools and Spares

The following is a general list of tools and spares that will see you through most eventualities on a tour. It's a good idea to take a good look at your bike and all the parts you may need to change, adjust or repair, and make sure you have a good quality tool to do each job.

If you will need to dismantle and reassemble your bike for transportation, make very sure you have everything you need for that as well.

You should take:

1. Two inner tubes, puncture repair kit, pump and tyre levers (metal, if possible)
2. Allen keys for all the allen bolts on your bike, socket spanners
3. Knife and/or scissors
4. Screwdrivers (2 or 3, flat blade and phillips)
5. Pliers
6. Chain breaker
7. Brake cables
8. Brake blocks/pads – or fit new ones before your tour starts
9. Spare spokes
10. Chain lube, oil
11. Cable ties, strong tape, string
12. Hand cleaner and/or wipes

Items 2 to 6 can be incorporated in one compact tool to save weight and space. You'll probably only need 3 or 4 allen keys and possibly no spanners. Many screws have dual heads so either type of screwdriver can be used.

Printed in Great Britain
by Amazon